COLLECTAFACT™

WORDS AND PICTURES — THAT WORK TOGETHER

OCEANS

TWO CAN™

PRINCETON ■ LONDON

What's in this book

*All words in the text which appear in **bold** can be found in the glossary*

Looking at the oceans

Over two–thirds of the world's surface is covered by vast oceans. They are the oldest and largest living **environments**. Life began in the oceans more than 3,500 million years ago. But, although oceans dominate the world map, we have only just begun to explore their hidden depths.

Without the **fertile** ocean, the Earth would be dry, barren, and devoid of life. Beneath its surface lie rugged mountains, active volcanoes, vast plateaus, and seemingly bottomless **trenches**. The deèpest ocean trenches could easily swallow up the tallest mountains on land!

Seen from above, the world's oceans appear empty and unchanging, but beneath the surface hides a unique world where water takes the place of air. A fantastic and rich mix of plants and animals live in these waters, from minute **plankton** to the giant blue whale, the largest **mammal** on Earth.

FastFact
The deepest parts of the ocean are under great pressure from the amount of water above them, and most creatures cannot survive here.

▶ Animals can travel freely through the water. Most sea animals breathe underwater, but some, such as dolphins and most whales, need to come up for air every few minutes.

◀ In the Tropics, the ocean are warm and clear. But around the North and Sou Poles it is very cold and pa of the ocean are always frozen. Huge chunks of ice called icebergs, float here.

Dividing the seas

In a way, there is really only one ocean. It stretches from the **North Pole** to the **South Pole** and encircles the globe. However, because **continents** divide this vast expanse of water, four separate oceans are recognized – the Pacific, the Atlantic, the Indian, and the Arctic. Within these oceans are smaller bodies of water called seas, **bays,** and **gulfs** that are cut off from the open oceans by land formations.

The Pacific is the largest and deepest of the four great oceans. It covers more of the world's surface than all the continents put together. The word Pacific means peaceful but the water can be very rough. Waves of up to 112ft tall have been recorded in the Pacific Ocean.

The Atlantic is the second biggest ocean, covering one–fifth of the world's surface. It is also the most important ocean for **commerce**, and therefore the busiest. Large boats regularly cross the Atlantic, carrying all types of cargo between the Americas, Africa, and Europe.

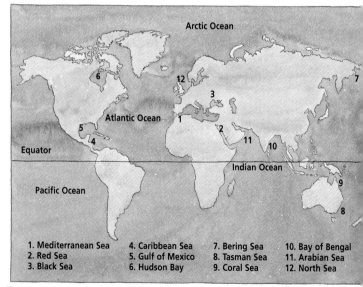

1. Mediterranean Sea	4. Caribbean Sea	7. Bering Sea	10. Bay of Bengal
2. Red Sea	5. Gulf of Mexico	8. Tasman Sea	11. Arabian Sea
3. Black Sea	6. Hudson Bay	9. Coral Sea	12. North Sea

DID YOU KNOW?

● It may take one drop of sea water 5,000 years to travel through all the world's oceans.

● The Atlantic Ocean is growing and the Pacific is shrinking. The continents move a couple of inches each year, so the relative sizes of the oceans are always changing.

● Greek divers are known to have reached depths of between 70ft and 100ft in search of treasures. When a diver ran short of breath, he would poke his head into a weighted diving bell filled with air.

astFact
About 200 million years ago, all the land on the Earth was joined together and one huge ocean stretched across the whole world.

▲ In warm, tropical seas, where the water is shallow and clear, there are vast, rocky structures known as coral reefs. These are made by small sea animals called polyps. Coral reefs hold a greater variety of life than any other part of the oceans.

Where are the seas and oceans?

The main oceans of the world – the Arctic, Pacific, Atlantic, Indian, and Antarctic – cover more than two-thirds of the Earth's surface. Seas are smaller and shallower than oceans. Some seas are inland, such as the Caspian Sea, a large salt water lake which lies between Southeast Europe and Western Asia. Oceans and seas provide us with many different things. Some contain rich sea life, some are important travel routes for **commerce** and trade, while the world's warmest waters provide lovely places to swim and play.

▲The Atlantic Ocean covers about a fifth of the Earth's surface, from North and South America to Europe and Africa, and is the most important for commerce.

▲The Indian Ocean stretches from Africa to Australia. It is the Earth's third largest ocean and its warm, **tropical** waters are home to a rich variety of sea life.

▲The Pacific Ocean is the largest and deepest ocean on Earth. It covers one-third of the Earth's surface, from Asia and Australia to North and South America.

▲The Arctic Ocean surrounds the **North Pole**. It is the smallest and shallowest ocean on Earth. Some **oceanographers** claim it is actually part of the Atlantic.

▲The Antarctic Ocean surrounds Antartica. Most oceanographers agree, however, that these waters are really part of the Atlantic, Pacific, and Indian oceans.

▲The Mediterranean Sea is the largest inland sea on Earth. It is surrounded by Europe to the north, Asia to the east, and Africa to the south.

◀ The Arctic and Antarctic waters are the coldest on Earth, and their inhabitants have adapted to this environment. Polar animals, such as penguins and seals, have developed extra layers of fat on their bodies to keep them warm.

The Bering Sea is the most northerly part of the Pacific Ocean. It lies between Alaska the US, and Siberia in Russia. It is named after the Danish explorer, Vitus Bering.

▲The Black Sea is an inland sea surrounded by Romania, Bulgaria, Turkey, and Russia and is connected to the Aegean Sea by the tiny Sea of Marmara.

▲The North Sea, part of the Atlantic Ocean, lies between Great Britain and northern Europe. Powerful **currents** and strong winds make this water unusually rough.

The Baltic Sea is a shallow gulf in the Atlantic Ocean. It is completely surrounded by land and is connected to the North Sea by two narrow channels.

▲The Caribbean Sea, part of the Atlantic Ocean between the West Indies and Central and South America, is warm and reaches a temperature of 90°F in summer.

▲The Gulf of Mexico lies in the Atlantic Ocean between Mexico, Cuba, and the US. Its many shallow areas and **marshy** coastline provide a few good harbors.

Moving waves

The world's oceans are always on the move. They travel in well-defined circular patterns called ocean **currents**. The currents flow like rivers, carrying warm water from the **Tropics** and cold water from the **Poles**. Where two currents meet, the colder water sinks, pushing warmer water up to the surface.

There is also the regular movement of **tides** in the seas and oceans. Twice a day, all over the world, oceans rise and fall along the coastlines. These tides are linked to the pull on the Earth by the Moon and the Sun.

Tides and currents carry food and stir the water, producing bubbles of **oxygen** which the sea animals breathe.

In the northern hemisphere, currents travel in a clockwise direction and in the southern hemisphere, they travel anti-clockwise.

FastFact
The distance that water reaches up a beach at high and low tide can be tiny, or as much as 52ft.

OCEAN POWER

● Giant whirlpools, or maelstroms, can occur in the oceans where two fast-rushing currents are forced through narrow channels.

● **Earthquakes** and volcanoes on the sea bed can cause huge waves to crash onto the shore. These giant waves are known as tidal waves, or **tsunamis**.

Food for life

Plants provide the basic food for life in the ocean, just as they do on land. Underwater plants are called **algae** and there are two main groups in the oceans.

The best known ocean algae are the seaweeds found around our coastlines. Limpets, periwinkles, and other shoreline creatures graze on seaweed, but these are not available to the animals of the open ocean.

The most important **marine** algae are called phytoplankton. These tiny, floating plants grow wherever sunlight penetrates the water. Huge clouds of phytoplankton drift in the upper layers of the ocean, but these are too small to be seen with the naked eye.

Floating alongside and feeding upon the phytoplankton are tiny animals called zooplankton. This rich mix of plant and animal life – called **plankton** – is the foundation of all marine life.

PLANKTON FACTS

● Sailors crossing the ocean at night often see a soft glow on the water's surface. This is because some plankton produce flashes of blue–green light when they are disturbed.

● Some early life forms probably looked like today's phytoplankton.

● The largest animals in the world feed on plankton. Blue whales can weigh over 100 tons and measure about 100ft long. They filter tiny shrimps – called krill – from the ocean, through a curtain of whalebone inside their mouths.

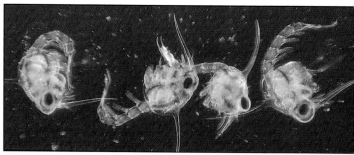

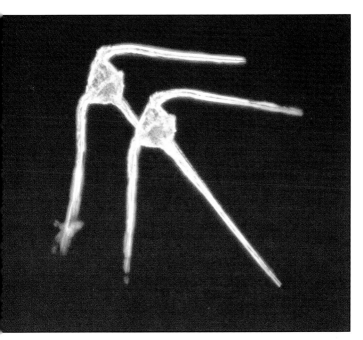

Many of the tiny
ting plants that form
phytoplankton join up
nake bracelets and
ns. Others float alone
look like small ice picks,
ons, or shells.

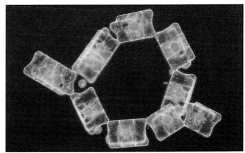

ome zooplankton are
le-celled life forms.
ers are the larvae of
or other sea animals.

All shapes and sizes

There is an amazing variety of animals living in the world's oceans. Their size, shape, and color varies enormously from creature to creature.

To some extent, each **marine** animal's appearance depends on its life style and the ocean **environment** in which it lives. Sea anemones and sponges, for instance, often stay rooted to the ocean floor all their lives and look more like plants than animals.

Fish are the most familiar marine creatures, but even their looks can be deceptive. Some species, such as eels, look more like snakes than fish. Others, such as the delicate sea horse, seem like a different kind of animal altogether.

▲ Many sea animals are a silvery–blue color, but sor have bright, bold markin The most colorful animals live in clear, tropical wate Their striking appearance helps them to establish territory and frighten off hungry predators.

◄ The octopus is one of many odd–looking sea animals. It has eight arms a short, rounded body, and lives on the ocean bed. To swim, octopuses squirt water from a speci siphon in their bodies.

▲ The waters near the bottom of the oceans are cold and dark. Many deep–sea creatures, such as this angler fish, have a light on their body that attracts prey.

here are over 3,500 species
marine sponge living on the
floor. Some form fleshy
ets, others look like upright
kestacks.

he blue–spotted stingray
osely related to the shark.
oats over the surface of
sea bed, feeding on slugs
worms.

Hunters and the hunted

A great number of **marine** animals spend their entire lives sifting the waters of our oceans and seas for **plankton** to feed on. However, they in turn are hunted by other animals. It is estimated that for every ten plankton–eaters, there is at least one hunter lurking nearby.

The shark is one of the most well-known and dangerous marine hunters. It is a perfectly designed killing machine. The shark's body is streamlined for a life of fast hunting and its mouth is lined with razor–sharp teeth.

Although they have a reputation as man–eaters, only 25 of the 200 varieties of shark are actually dangerous to people. Sharks spend most of their time racing through the water in pursuit of their **prey** fish, seals, turtles, small whales, other shar and even some sea birds.

Not all marine hunters are as fearsome a sharks. The pretty sea anemones may look harmless, but they trap animals in their feathery tentacles. They inject venom into their victims, in a similar way to jellyfish.

DEFENSE FACTS

● Octopuses and cuttlefish defend themselves by squirting ink into the faces of their attackers, giving themselves time to get away.

● Many sea animals, such as clams, live in shells. These act as armor, protecting the animal's soft body from **predators**.

● Flying fish leap out of the water to escape their enemies.

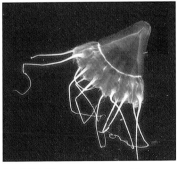

▲ Jellyfish, like sea anemones, catch prey in their trailing tentacles and sting them. Some of the most powerful poisons in the natural world are produced by jellyfish!

◄ Even when sharks are not chasing their next meal, they must keep moving all the time or they begin to sink.

Taking to the water

During the long passage of time, a small procession of land animals has returned to the oceans for its livelihood. Reptiles, mammals, and even birds have braved the deep, salty waters to take advantage of the rich bounty of sea life.

Whales, seals, turtles, and penguins are some of the animals that have left dry land to colonize the oceans. Although they may spend most of their time in the sea, these creatures cannot breathe underwater like true sea animals, so they regularly visit the water's surface for air.

Whales are the most successful ocean colonizers. People often mistake them for fish, as whales spend their entire lives in the water. However, most animals that have taken to the water must come back on land to **reproduce**.

FastFact
Sperm whales can dive deeper than any other mammal, to over 9,000ft, but must swim to the surface regularly for air.

▲ Sea birds usually live on coastlines or on remote islands, but penguins spend more time than most sea birds actually swimming in the cold waters.

Polar bears are marine mammals that spend most of their time on or in the frozen Arctic Ocean, hunting seals. Expert swimmers, their wide, furry paws are webbed to help them swim more easily.

Sea reptiles, such as turtles, are found in the warmer seas of the world. They lay their eggs on sandy beaches.

Ocean resources

People cannot live in the world's oceans but they have always harvested their rich waters. As the human population has grown, people have turned to the oceans more and more to increase their supply of food and raw materials. Today, over 150 billion pounds of fish are caught each year, and around one–fifth of the world's **oil** and **gas** is mined from the sea bed.

Modern fishing methods are often so effective that they devastate fish communities and upset the balance of sea life. Many formerly **fertile** seas are no longer able to support large fishing fleets because the fish populations are so low.

The nets used by many of today's fishermen can also cause problems. They are made of nylon and do not rot underwater. If they are lost overboard, these nets become death traps to seals, dolphins and other **marine** creatures that cannot detect them.

astFact
ome fishing nets are several
niles long and can catch more
han 100 million fish at a time.

t is not only fish, such as cod and herring,
at are in demand. Crabs and lobsters are
o popular seafood products. In addition,
me whales and seals have been hunted to
tinction for their meat, oil, or fur.

**This North Sea trawler is small compared
the supertrawlers, which can be more
n 290ft long.**

OCEAN PRODUCTS

● Fish oils are used to make glues, soaps, and margarines.

● A rare gem called a **pearl** is formed inside the shells of certain oysters.

● Big deposits of iron, copper, and **manganese** are lifted from the sea bed using suction pumps, or are raked into nets by dredging machines.

● In dry areas, sea water is sometimes treated to create a fresh water supply.

● Seaweed can be eaten like a vegetable and is also used to make ice cream, toothpaste, paints, and other everyday products.

Making the sea sick

Although we rely on the world's oceans for food, in reality we treat them like dumpsites. Waste is pumped and dumped into the water and **pesticides** and other manufactured **pollutants** are washed into the ocean by rivers and streams.

The pollution of the world's oceans is harmful. Many sea animals are injured, strangled, or suffocated each year because of floating debris called flotsam. The high level of toxic wastes in a few seas and oceans is poisoning some animals and driving others away.

The **land–locked** seas, such as the Mediterranean, are among the most polluted of the world's waters.

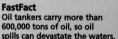

FastFact
Oil tankers carry more than 600,000 tons of oil, so oil spills can devastate the waters.

▲ Oil spills threaten marine life. This sea bird will probably die unless the oil is cleaned from its feathers.

POLLUTION PROBLEMS

● Sealed barrels of dangerous radioactive and chemical waste have been dumped in some oceans, but we do not know if these containers are safe in these watery conditions.

● In some places around the world, pollution of the oceans has made local seafood unfit to eat.

Busy ports can become deserted. The oil, sewage, and litter spilled into the water makes a harbor unfit for sea life.

DOS H^{nos} GUERRERO
CU 1568

Save the oceans

People all over the world are beginning to realize the importance of the oceans. International laws have been made to restrict the amount of waste put into the water, and some **marine mammals** are now protected.

Countries on the shores of the dirtiest seas have begun clean-up programs. But there is still a lot to be done.

In recent years, enormous damage has been caused in some oceans by oil tankers spilling their deadly cargo. Oil spills on the water's surface block out light from the Sun. This upsets **plankton** production under the water and affects all marine life. Through public pressure, oil companies could be persuaded to buy safer boats that would not leak in an accident.

Activities that were once considered to be harmless have now been found to have damaging effects on marine life. The electric cables lying on the ocean floor disturb some sea bed creatures and confuse many fish. Some sharks bite into the cables, mistaking them for **prey**.

The noisy hustle and bustle from boats, busy coastal resorts, and ocean-based industries frighten away seals, dolphins, and other animals from their breeding grounds.

Whales – the giants of the natural world – have been hunted for their oils and meat for so long that they are now difficult to find. As a result, they have become a strong international symbol of ocean **conservation**.

Most people agree that we must not kill any more whales and laws have now been passed to protect the largest whale species. But, sadly, a few countries continue to hunt whales and people eat their meat as an expensive delicacy.

Dakuwaca fights for his life

This tale is told by the people of Fiji, who depend on the ocean for food and transport.

Long ago, sharks were the rulers of the islands that make up Fiji in the Pacific Ocean. Each island had its own particular shark who lived beside the reef entrance to the island. These sharks patrolled the waters of their territory, challenging anyone who dared to come near. They allowed friends through, but fought with hostile sharks until they paid a tribute.

Dakuwaca thought himself the greatest of all the sharks. He was big and fierce and enjoyed nothing better than a fight with another shark. He had never lost a fight and he was sure he never would.

He didn't care about the terrible storms which his fights caused, whipping up the waters so that the islanders were tossed about in their boats. Often island houses were swept away by massive waves from the ocean.

Dakuwaca was patrolling his reef one day when he came across a shark called Masilica. Masilica was the mischief maker among the sharks. He did not fight much himself but, with his wily ways, he had caused more fights than most sharks had fought!

"Good day, Dakuwaca," he said. "I suppose you're eager for another fight. It's amazing, the way you always beat the other sharks. I wish I were as good a fighter as you."

"No other shark is as good a fighter as I am," said Dakuwaca. "Hardly anyone bothers to challenge me any more. They all know that I am so much stronger than them. In fact, it's getting very dull around here."

"Perhaps if you really want a good fight you should go over to Kandavu Island. I hear there's a creature well worth fighting there, a mighty monster which guards the reef so that it is impossible to go near it. But no one ever goes there because they are too afraid," said Masilica, with a sly glint in his eye.

"Of course, I'm not suggesting that you're frightened – you're much too brave. And I'm sure none of the other sharks think that you're afraid either."

Dakuwaca thrashed his tail through the water. Of course he wasn't afraid, what a suggestion! But if the other sharks thought he was afraid, he had better do something at once. Almost before Masilica had finished speaking, Dakuwaca set off toward the island of Kandavu, determined to challenge the fearsome monster.

As Dakuwaca approached Kandavu, he heard a deep, powerful voice calling from the shore. Dakuwaca had never heard anything like it before and he found himself trembling a little.

"How foolish," he told himself. "Nothing on the shore can harm me." And he swam on.

"Stop!" commanded the powerful voice. "I am Tui Vesi, the guardian of Kandavu. How dare you approach my precious island so boldly."

Dakuwaca was frightened, but was determined not to show it. "And I am Dakuwaca, the greatest of all sharks," he said. "Come out and fight to defend your island."

"I am a land guardian and so cannot come into the water to fight you," said Tui Vesi. "I shall send one of my servants to fight you instead. But be warned! It is a great and terrible monster, and it would be much better if you left now."

28

"No one is braver or stronger than I," said [D]akuwaca. "I am not afraid of anything. I [will] fight your servant."

[H]e swam around the mouth of the reef, [wa]tching and waiting for his opponent. His [bo]dy was strong and quick and his teeth [we]re sharp.

[S]uddenly, a giant arm appeared from the [ree]f and grabbed him. A giant octopus! This [wa]sn't what Dakuwaca was expecting at all!

He thrashed and twisted to rid himself of the arm. His sharp teeth were quite useless because he could not bend his body to bite at the arm. The arm loosened as he twisted and, for a moment, Dakuwaca thought he was finally free.

But no, two more arms whipped round so that he could no longer move at all. And the arms began to squeeze, tighter and tighter, until Dakuwaca could bear it no longer.

"Have mercy," Dakuwaca gasped. "Forgive my terrible presumption, Tui Vesi."

The arms of the giant octopus loosened slightly, and Tui Vesi's mighty voice boomed out into the waters once more.

"I will release you, Dakuwaca, providing that you promise to guard the people of my island from sharks which might attack them when they go out fishing in their canoes."

"Yes, yes! Of course I will," Dakuwaca agreed.

At once the octopus released Dakuwaca a he sank to the sea bed exhausted. When had recovered, he set off back to his own territory. From that day onward, he kept promise and protected the island of Kand from other sharks.

In spite of his fears, the other sharks believed his claim that he had made frien with the mighty guardian of Kandavu anc feared Dakuwaca just as much as before. All except Masilica, that is, who would occasionally drop the word 'octopus' into conversation and dash away as Dakuwaca snapped at him.

And that is why, while other fishermen the Fiji islands fear for their lives because the sharks, the men of Kandavu ride safel and happily in their canoes.

True or false?

Which of these facts are true and which are false?
If you have read this book carefully, you will know the answers!

1. Almost one-third of the world's surface is covered by oceans.

2. The paws of a polar bear are webbed.

3. Dolphins and whales can stay underwater for several hours.

4. Sound travels through water five times faster than through air.

5. The world's four oceans are the Pacific, the Atlantic, the Aegean, and the Mediterranean.

6. It takes 5,000 years for one drop of seawater to travel through all the world's oceans.

7. **Tsunamis** are caused by underwater volcanic explosions and **earthquakes**.

8. **Plankton** is a rich mixture made up of the debris from seaweed.

9. Octopuses have 12 arms and feed mainly on seals.

10. Seaweed is used to make ice cream.

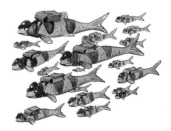

11. Fish travel in schools until they have learnt how to protect themselves.

12. Sharks must keep moving all the time or they will sink.

ANSWERS: 1.F 2.T 3.F 4.T 5.F 6.T 7.T 8.F 9.F 10.T 11.F 12.T

Parts of a fish

There are more than 20,000 species of fish, many of which have a number of features in common. They breathe through gills, and have long, streamlined bodies for easy movement through the water. They use their fins for steering and balancing. Scales all over their bodies can be used as defense against **predators**.

▼ **Dorsal Fin**
Dorsal fins are found on the back of a fish. Cod are unusual because they have three dorsal fins, while most other fish have only two. The dorsal fins help the fish to stay upright in the water.

▶ **Lateral Line**
Almost all fish have an invisible line along each side of their body, from head to tail. This is a special sense organ called the lateral line. Nerve cells along this line react to even the smallest change in the temperature, pressure, or movement of the water, so the fish can detect an approaching predator before it comes into view.

▶ **Caudal Fin**
The tail fin is also called the caudal fin. The fish pushes itself through the water by swinging this fin from side to side. The caudal fin is also used for steering.

▲ **Anal Fins**
Like the dorsal fins, the anal fins help the fish to balance in the water and stop it rolling from side to side. Cod are unusual because they have two anal fins, whereas most fish only have one.

▼ Pectoral Fin
Pectoral fins are found on the side of a fish's body. They are used for steering and stopping.

▼ Scales
Scales are made of a thin, bone-like layer and form a protective covering around the fish's body. Most, but not all, fish have scales. Scales are colorless – markings on a fish's body are caused by cells in its skin.

► Barbels
Some fish, including cod, have whisker-like feelers on their mouths called barbels. They are used to taste and touch things.

●elvic Fin
●e pair of fins on the underside of   fish are called pelvic fins or ventral s. They are used for steering and oping. The position of the pelvic varies from one species of fish to ●ther. The pelvic fins on a cod are ●ont of its pectoral fins, but some have pelvic fins next to their tail.

▲ Gills
Most fish have four gills on either side of their heads, each made up of tiny filaments. To breathe, the fish sucks in water through the mouth. When it closes its mouth, water is squeezed out through the gills. As it passes through the gills, oxygen in the water is absorbed by the filaments, and carbon dioxide is released into the water. Blood then carries oxygen around the fish's body. The gills are protected by a cover called the operculum.

astFact
●d is an important source of ●od from the oceans – we eat ●ore cod than any other fish!

Glossary

A substance that is **acidic** tastes sharp and bitter, like vinegar.

Algae are plants that grow underwater, such as seaweeds.

An **axis** is a real or imaginary line on which an object can rotate, or turn, such as the Earth, which spins constantly on its axis.

A **bay** is part of an ocean or other large body of water that forms a curve in the shoreline. It is bordered on the coastline by capes or headlands (high ridges of land jutting out over water).

Carbon dioxide is a gas which is formed in the body and released by the lungs every time humans or animals breathe out. Plants are able to use carbon dioxide for growth and produce oxygen.

Cells are the tiny living organisms that all living matter is made up of, including the human body.

Commerce is another word for business.

Conservation is the preservation of species and environments from damage by humans. This involves asking parliament to make environmental laws and put pressure companies to take care of the environment. A number of organisations are dedicated to this cause, for example, Greenpeace.

A **continent** is one of the seven main masses of land on Earth, such as Asia and Africa.

A **coral reef** is a ridge formation found underwater. It is made up of the skeletons of millions of tiny animals called polyps.

A **current** or stream is the movement of body of water in a particular direction. Ocean currents may be very strong and extend over great distances.

Earthquakes are created when a success of vibrations shake the Earth's surface a

use it to break up. Earthquakes can cause
widespread destruction on land and tidal
waves in the oceans.

echo is the repetition of a noise caused
by the bouncing back of sound waves from
solid object. Marine mammals, such as
dolphins, use echoes to locate food and
avoid obstacles.

Land-locked areas of water are surrounded
by land. Some small seas, such as the
Caspian Sea, are land-locked.

Mammals, such as humans, bats, mice, cats,
and dolphins, are warm-blooded animals
that feed their young on mother's milk.

environment is the particular set of
conditions in an area, such as climate
and surroundings, that affects the living
things that inhabit it. An animal's survival
depends on how well it is able to respond
to these conditions.

extinction occurs when the last member of
species dies out. This may be due to over-
hunting by humans, the arrival of a rival
animal or plant, or environmental changes.

being fertile is being able to produce life and
being rich in the things that support animal
plant life, such as minerals and water.

is is a substance which will change shape
fill any container.

Gulf is the part of a sea or an ocean that
dips into the neighboring coastline. It is
narrower at its mouth than a bay.

Islands are areas of land that are completely
surrounded by water and can vary in size
up to 1,351,068 square miles, the size
Greenland.

Manganese is a brittle, greyish-white
metallic element, often used in the making
of steel.

Marine means "connected with the sea."
Marine animals and plants are those which
live in the sea.

Marshlands are areas of land that are a
mixture of water and land. Some marshlands can be walked through because the
water is so shallow, but some may need to
be reached by boat, such as the Everglades
in the US state of Florida.

Minerals are chemical compounds found
in rocks. Some of them, such as copper,
iron, and uranium, are useful to humans
and are mined.

Molten rock is hot, melted rock, such as the lava that comes out of volcanoes. It is what the Earth was made of when it was formed.

Oceanographers are scientists who study the seas and oceans.

Oil is a greasy liquid derived from animals, plants, and mineral deposits. It is processed by humans for use as fuel, soaps, glues, and foods such as margarine.

Oxygen is the gas that we breathe in constantly which is essential for human, plant, and animal life. Plants need carbon dioxide by day and oxygen by night to reproduce and grow.

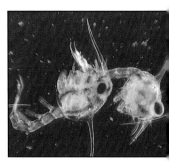

Photosynthesis is where plants use the Sun's energy to turn water and carbon dioxide into food.

Plankton is a rich mixture of many types of microscopic life, such as phytoplankton and zooplankton. It is important to marine life because many sea animals feed on it.

The **poles** are found at the exact north and south ends of the Earth and are known as the North Pole and South Pole. The weather is mostly cold and six months of the year are spent in darkness here.

A **pearl** is a small gem, usually round and white, cream-colored, or bluish-gray. It slowly forms as a protective layer around a grain of sand or other object that irritates the soft flesh inside an oyster's shell.

Pesticides are chemicals used to kill pests that feed on crops. Some may be dangerous to other creatures too.

pollutant is a poisonous product, such as fumes or oil, that damages the environment, causing harm to plants and animals.

predators are animals, such as sharks and polar bears, which eat other animals. **Prey** are animals that are eaten by other animals.

reproduction is when adult creatures produce young to continue their species.

reptiles are cold-blooded creatures which have scaly skin, such as snakes and lizards.

seiches (pronounced say-shez) are storm waves that move up and down on the surface of the ocean.

species is a group of animals that are closely related to one another, such as killer whales, and are therefore able to breed.

surf is the white part of the sea created on land near the beach when waves reach land and pile on top of each other.

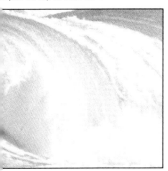

Swell is the name for storm waves that move across the ocean.

Tides occur when the sea rises and falls due to the pull of the Moon and the Sun on the Earth's surface.

Toxic substances are poisonous and harmful to life.

A **trench** is a deep furrow. The Mariana Trench near Guam is the deepest known place in any ocean.

The **Tropic of Cancer** and the **Tropic of Capricorn** are imaginary lines found at about 23 degrees latitude north and south of the equator. The Tropics are the warmest places on Earth.

A **tsunami** is a huge sea wave caused by an underwater earthquake or volcanic eruption.

Water vapor is the substance created when water warms and is released into the atmosphere to cause clouds and mist.

Activity space

Photocopy this sheet and use it to make your own notes.

Photocopy this sheet and use it to make your own notes.

Draw your own ocean scene

Questions and answers

For frank answers you need Frank Fish! He will answer all the questions you probably have about seas and oceans. Bubbles the Sea horse is also full of questions...

How were the oceans formed?
Scientists believe that the Earth was formed about 4,600 million years ago and at first it was a mass of **molten rock**. As the molten rock on the surface bubbled and boiled, it released **water vapor** into the atmosphere. This created clouds, and the clouds created rain! Over time, the planet cooled down enough for the rain to form puddles. As more rain fell, the puddles turned into ponds, the ponds gradually turned into lakes, the lakes into seas and the seas into an ocean! The water in the first ocean was not salty but **acidic**, like vinegar, and very hot.

What's the difference between a sea and an ocean?
A sea is salt water that is partly or completely surrounded by land.

Sea horses use their tails as anchors and hook them around weeds or coral to avoid being swept away by underwater currents.

Bubbles the Sea horse

An ocean is the expanse of salt water that stretches between two **continents**. Some s are called **gulfs** or **bays**. Usually, a gulf is bigger than a bay, but there are exceptior

Why is sea water salty?
Everyone knows that sea water tastes salty On average, 2.2lb of water from the ocean contains 1oz of salt. The salt in the sea actually comes from the earth and rocks ir the ground. Soil contains lots of minerals, including salts. Every time it rains some of these minerals get washed away. The salts dissolved in the rain are collected by rivers and the rivers carry them to the sea.

Why is sea water saltier than river wat
The amount of salt in river water is tiny because rivers carry most of their salt to th sea. Water from the sea and from large la is evaporated by heat from the Sun. Wher salt water turns to vapor, it leaves its salt behind. Over millions of years, as water ha evaporated from the oceans and seas, the amount of salt has gradually increased. Tropical waters are very salty because the Sun is warmer there and more water is evaporated. Melting icebergs dilute the co water at the poles, making the water less sa

What causes waves in the ocean?
Most waves are caused by the wind blowir across the surface of the oceans. A gentle breeze will cause tiny ripples on the water Hurricanes and typhoons can create might waves that are more than 90ft high.

...e there different types of waves?

...ere are two main types of waves caused ...high winds. "**Seiches**" (pronounced say-...z) move up and down, while "**swell**" ...ves across the ocean. The swell created by ...torm can travel hundreds or thousands of ...es. As the waves approach the shore, the ...tance between each wave gets shorter ...d the waves pile up on each other until ...y topple over. This is why waves break, ...ming surf on the beaches.

...at is a tidal wave?

...e typhoons and hurricanes, underground ...thquakes can cause powerful waves, ...etimes called tidal waves, or **tsunamis**, ...ch can be up to 280ft high. In the open ...an, tsunamis appear as tiny ripples ...ng across the water at speeds of up to ...m/h – as fast as a jumbo jet! As these ...les approach the shore, they pile up and ...m a single enormous wave which can ...se widespread destruction.

...at are tides?

...es are the constantly changing levels in ... Earth's waters. We can see these changes ...he level that sea water reaches up to on ...shores. Sometimes the water rises far up ...beach, other times it stays much further ...ay. In most places, the tide rises and falls ...e a day. Some places have only one tide, ...le others have three. The size of a tide ...es, from too small to measure to as much ...0ft, depending on where it is and the ...e of year.

Fish are vertebrates, which have animals that have a backbone. Multi-colored fish are able to hide in coral reefs and catch prey.

Frank Fish

What makes the level of sea water change to cause tides?

The Moon spins around the Earth and produces a force. Water on the side of the Earth nearest the Moon is pulled up by this force – creating a high tide. At the same time, at the other side of the world, there is another bulge of water – caused by the force of the Earth turning on its axis – and another high tide. As the Earth and Moon spin around, these bulges of water move about. This causes tides to come in to shore and go out again all over the world.

What are the main layers of the ocean?

The top layers of the ocean are the sublittoral and euphotic zones. Most sea creatures live here as they are reached by sunlight, allowing plants to **photosynthesize**. Below the euphotic zone is the bathyal zone, where there is little or no light. Fish that live here are often able to produce light with their bodies. The vast ocean depths are called the abyssal zone, where only a few creatures can survive in this icy cold and pitch-black environment. The deepest level – the hadal zone – supports few life forms.

Index

Published by
Two-Can Publishing LLC
234 Nassau Street
Princeton, NJ 08542

www.two-canpublishing.com

Copyright © 2001, Two-Can Publishing

For information on Two-Can books and multimedia,
call 1-609-921-6700, fax 1-609-921-3349, or visit
our Web site at http://www.two-canpublishing.com

Author: Lucy Baker
Consultant: Simon Wakefield

"Two-Can" is a trademark of Two-Can Publishing
Two-Can Publishing is a division of Zenith Entertainment
43–45 Dorset Street, London, W1H 4AB

Hardback ISBN 1-58728-756-0
Hardback 1 2 3 4 5 6 7 8 9 10 02 01

Photograph Credits: Ace Photo Agency: front cover
Ardea/Clem Haagner: p.2, p.9; Greenpeace/Morgan: p
Ardea/François Gohier: p.5; Ardea/Ron & Valerie Taylor:
p.7, p.34, p.37, p.47; ZEFA/Dr D James: p.10–11; Plan
Earth/Robert Arnold: p.12, p.36; Oxford Scientific
Films/Peter Parks: p.13 (top & bottom); Ardea/J-M Lab
p.14 (top;) Oxford Scientific Films/GI Bernard: p.14
(bottom); Planet Earth/Peter David: p.15 (top left); Pla
Earth/Gillian Lythgoe: p15 (top right); Planet Earth/Pe
Scoones: p.15 (bottom); Ardea/Ron & Valerie Taylor:
Planet Earth/Peter David: p.17; Ardea/Clem Haagner: p
Planet Earth: Ardea/Jim Brandenberg: p.19 (top);
Ardea/François Gohier: p.19 (bottom); B&C Alexande
p.20–21; Ardea/Richard Vaughan: p.22; ZEFA: p.23;
Ardea/François Gohier: p.24–25. Illustrations on pag
8–9, 32–33, and 44–45 are by Dai Owen, James Jarvi
Stuart Trotter, Nick Ward, and Simon Woolford.
All other Illustrations are by Francis Mosley

Reproduced by Next Century, Hong Kong
Printed by Wing King Tong, Hong Kong

This title previously published in a large format.